SERENITY @ WORK

SERENITY @ WORK

How to Surrender Control, Establish and Maintain Serenity @ Work

Maureen Lombardo

Serenity @ Work How to Surrender Control, Establish and Maintain Serenity @ Work Copyright © 2018 by Maureen Lombardo

All rights reserved. No part of this publication may be reproduced, distributed, or transmitted in any form or by any means, including photocopying, recording, or other electronic or mechanical methods, without the prior written permission of the author, except in the case of brief quotations embodied in critical reviews and certain other noncommercial uses permitted by copyright law.

Jones Media Publishing
10645 N. Tatum Blvd. Ste. 200-166
Phoenix, AZ 85028
www.JonesMediaPublishing.com

Printed in the United States of America

ISBN-13: 978-1-945849-51-0

DEDICATION

To Michele and Karen, thanks for
all that you've taught me

CONTENTS

INTRODUCTION 1
FINDING A WAY TO SURRENDER @ WORK 9
ESTABLISHING YOUR SERENITY @ WORK 19
THE FREEDOM OF FORGIVENESS @ WORK .. 31
FAKE IT 'TIL YOU MAKE IT @ WORK 51
MAINTAINING YOUR SERENITY @ WORK 57
BE OF SERVICE @ WORK 67
SET BOUNDARIES @ WORK 73
WHAT HAPPENS NEXT? 77

INTRODUCTION

THIS BOOK WILL SERVE ANYONE interested in beginning a journey of self-discovery that can help you let go of the things that hold you back from being your best and most authentic self. I'd like to share with you the steps I took and am still revisiting. My journey had its origins in the work I did in the 12 Steps of the Alcoholics Anonymous program. As I have met and worked with the AA fellowship, we in recovery have discussed how beneficial the 12 step work can be to everyone. You do not have to be suffering from addiction to be empowered by the process of surrendering control and establishing and maintaining serenity, helping you become your best and most authentic self. Letting go of resentments, fear and self-delusion makes way for honesty, humility and selflessness. As such, you open yourself to others as a free and joyous person. You no longer seek to control or influence the behavior of others, but instead have the inner power to control your reactions to people and circumstances that inevitably impact you every day at home and @ Work. So, to that end............

"I'm Maureen and I'm an alcoholic." At the time of this writing, I have been saying those words for eight years. Long before I took ownership of these words, the people in my life had been thinking: "This is Maureen and, God help us, she is an alcoholic."

At a recent meeting a fellow alcoholic said something that struck me: "I don't come to these meetings to try to live without drinking, I come to these meetings to live with sobriety." The statement was powerful to me because many alcoholics agree that not taking a drink is very straightforward. It is not easy, but it is clear. Do not drink. Do not use your drug of choice. Early into my sobriety, I was like, "Cool, done...Wait, why don't I feel better?" Not drinking or using is a critical step, but it is just the first step. Learning how to live this new life without the impacts of alcohol is what is really challenging. That is where working the 12 Steps of Alcoholics Anonymous means the difference between true serenity versus living a life without alcohol but still having all the anger. Living a life without alcohol but still having all the fear. Living a life without alcohol but still having all the resentment.

As I worked the steps and began to unpack all the things that had kept me in that prison, I became less angry. I became less fearful, less resentful and less likely to freak out on the people in my life. Serenity has been an amazing gift for my spirituality and family, a foundation that fortifies. It allows me to be at my best and most authentic self. Originally, I began the work so that I could stay sober and find joy in my life. As I worked toward that joy and serenity, I found that when I was able to embrace my true and authentic self, not only did my life and relationships improve. My work improved, too. I had not considered or anticipated the positive impact on my professional life. In retrospect, it makes so much sense. When we are joyous, that spirit spills into our whole life. When I found serenity, I also found Serenity @ Work. That journey and my mistakes along the way are what I want to share in these chapters.

The wonderful state of Serenity @ Work is the only way I want to work. I know this because I have been on the other side. I have been the angry and resentful one @ Work. After working the steps and continuing to recognize when I have made a mistake and promptly admitted it, I feel less angry, less resentful, more at peace. It was not enough to not lose my cool with someone @ Work; I wanted to get to the place where I have no inclination to lose it with someone. That is a profound difference. And, for me, not easily achieved. But, with the graceful guidance of God and the AA program, each day now brings peace and possibility.

You do not need to be in recovery to benefit from these steps or thoughts. You just need to be like most of us, spending your workdays interacting with other people. People with talents, opinions and quirks. Things that have driven us all crazy at one time or another.

The Twelve Steps of Alcoholics Anonymous have helped ease many forms of addiction: drugs, gambling, overeating, overspending, sex and more. I believe these steps can be applied further to a life without addiction to help us get to know ourselves and work through the underlying hurts and resentments that cause us to lash out.

The Twelve Steps of Alcoholics Anonymous:

1. We admitted we were powerless over alcohol — that our lives had become unmanageable.
2. Came to believe that a Power greater than ourselves could restore us to sanity.
3. Made a decision to turn our will and our lives over to the care of God as we understood Him.
4. Made a searching and fearless moral inventory of ourselves.
5. Admitted to God, to ourselves and to another human being the exact nature of our wrongs.
6. Were entirely ready to have God remove all these defects of character.
7. Humbly asked Him to remove our shortcomings.
8. Made a list of all persons we had harmed, and became willing to make amends to them all.

9. Made direct amends to such people wherever possible, except when to do so would injure them or others.
10. Continued to take personal inventory and when we were wrong promptly admitted it.
11. Sought through prayer and meditation to improve our conscious contact with God, as we understood Him, praying only for knowledge of His will for us and the power to carry that out.
12. Having had a spiritual awakening as the result of these steps, we tried to carry this message to alcoholics, and to practice these principles in all our affairs.

If you are a normal drinker and otherwise free of addiction, reading these steps may feel like wasteful exercise. You don't suffer from addiction, therefore, what purpose can these words and steps have in your life? Indulge me and read them again after considering these questions about you and your work life:

- Do you ever feel like you have to have control over every aspect of your work to be successful?

- Do you ever feel like all the weight of a project or initiative is on you and only you?
- Do you ever feel like your leader, your customers and your teammates would be fine if they just listened to you?
- Do you ever feel you are up against everyone else @ Work?
- Do you ever feel like they just do not get you?

If you are like me, you answered "Yes" to at least one of these questions! Perhaps you answered "Yes" to more than one. Now, take the word "alcohol" out of the first step and consider a journey of self-discovery and demand for honesty in all of the steps. Applying these steps to how you approach your work can give you a sense of freedom and empowerment to help you achieve Serenity @ Work. In the next several chapters, I want to look at these steps in the groupings that speak to me as an effective methodology to becoming your best and most authentic self. There are three phases: Surrendering Control, Establishing Serenity and Maintaining Serenity. The first three of the 12 Steps are about recognizing that we need to address something. There is a calling within us to recognize that our lives are out of our control and that we need to gaze outward to help ourselves. To a great extent, we need to Surrender Control to gain the strength needed to go on and address what is driving our anger and resentments. Next, we need to Establish Serenity. Steps four, five, six and seven of the 12 Steps are about looking to self in a way that forces us to recognize the part we play in our pain and dysfunction. This calls for openness and honesty—the most brutal but rewarding honesty. We can then step outside ourselves in Steps eight and nine to reach out to those we have hurt and to make our amends. In previous Steps, we forgive ourselves. In Steps eight and nine we reach out to others for forgiveness. The process of Establishing Serenity frees us from this baggage of the past and allows us to move forward with a cleanliness earned by hard work and honesty. Finally, Steps 10, 11 and 12 give us the tools to keep our newly found serenity and pay it forward to friends and colleagues. In this way we Maintain Serenity.

FINDING A WAY TO SURRENDER @ WORK

IT IS IMPORTANT TO REALIZE that our lives are not in our complete control. We do not have nor do we need to always be in control. Having the ultimate control of every aspect of your life and your work is a concept many of us spend a painful amount of time chasing. Think of the arrogance it takes to assume that you have all the answers. There is a degree of delusion to think you alone can address everything without help.

There is a benefit in surrendering to the chaos of life. By surrendering, I do not mean to give up. What I mean is to free ourselves of the burden of taking everything on by ourselves. Life and work are messy, complicated and wonderful. Rather than fighting the chaos and trying to control it, it is so much healthier to acknowledge and enjoy it. We can't control what happens in our life but we can have a say in how we react to it. Work is like that, too. At work there are things over which we have control by nature of our position of direct authority. There are also things over which we can exert a good deal of influence based on our relationships and expertise. But there are things that affect us over which we have absolutely no control. I spent the majority of my pre-AA life turning myself inside out trying to change things I could not control, or reacting to them and making certain all of those around me knew how wrong it all was and how it should be fixed. I may not have always been externally boorish about it, but this reaction affected me and diminished my ability to be at my best in my work life. I carried a heavy resentment and anxiousness that negatively affected me and my relationships @ Work.

Now that I have admitted my wonderful powerlessness and celebrate a delicious vulnerability, I face those things I can't influence or control with a view toward how

I can make a challenging situation better for myself and those with whom I work. Certainly, if I were to come across a situation that is ethically wrong or illegal, I would follow the policies and procedures in place to do what I am responsible for doing. But I would not take it on as a crusade for which I alone knew the answer. This is a big difference. We do what we can in a spirit of integrity and good will, but what a gift it is to ourselves to not try to delude ourselves into thinking we alone can and should solve every problem.

When we recognize that we do not and cannot control everything ourselves, to whom do we turn for help? The journey toward serenity calls for us to identify and look to our higher power. Recognizing that our lives are out of our complete control helps us to acknowledge that there is a power greater than ourselves that can restore us to sanity. For many, this power is God. For me as a Catholic and specifically, a Franciscan, I look to the Holy Trinity as the power greater than myself. The 12 Steps are very clear, though, that atheists and agnostics can benefit from this process without having to embrace organized religion or a traditional view of a Judeo Christian God or any other deity. The idea transcends the notion of religion because we are called to recognize a power greater than ourselves. We are not the center. We do not have all the answers. There is a power that exceeds our own. I have heard atheists and agnostics in meetings share that the power they look to is nature or the universe. They are able to step away from themselves as being the center and having the answers.

That greater power, we recognize, can restore us to sanity. We don't and we can't do it alone. We truly surrender to our higher power by turning our will, our concerns and our lives over to a higher power of our own understanding. For me this surrendering was so freeing because I allowed myself to ask for help. I let go completely and allowed myself to be guided by a will outside of myself. I gained a great deal of strength from the Third Step Prayer:

From page 63 of the Big Book of Alcoholics Anonymous

God, I offer myself to Thee-
To build with me
and to do with me as Thou wilt.
Relieve me of the bondage of self,

> that I may better do Thy will.
> Take away my difficulties,
> that victory over them may bear witness
> to those I would help of Thy Power,
> Thy Love, and Thy Way of life.
> May I do Thy will always!

Again, these thoughts are less about pointing in a direction toward prayer and my faith, and more about considering how Surrendering Control can help us better deal with the challenges we face @ Work. Let's explore this prayer. What I believe the text calls us to do is to let go of the idea that we are the center of everything. I love the thought of letting go of the "bondage of self". Being self-centered weighs us down. Every burden we take on without looking outside of ourselves for help and guidance adds an additional link to the chain of self-absorption we carry with us. It's a burden and makes us angry and resentful. I benefit from handing that chain to my higher power and asking for help with it all. I also allow myself to reach out to my colleagues and teammates for help and guidance. When I fully embraced the fact that I am not at the center of things, I finally felt free. The weight of the world does not rest on my shoulders. I am not alone. I alone do not have to solve everything. I can surrender to my higher power's will for me and seek to understand it.

Applying this concept @ Work can free us of the immense pressure we put on ourselves to solve every problem and seek perfection. In addition to looking to our higher power, we can and should call upon our support network @ Work. We have teammates, business partners and customers. How can we look at the opportunity at hand and engage with our network to arrive at a great result?

It takes humility to ask for help. Humility can be mistakenly associated with weakness. I disagree. To be humble is not to be weak. There is a self-awareness and confidence needed to open our defenses and ask for help.

An important factor in successfully engaging our network @ Work is to trust in that network. We need to build and cultivate our work relationships based on a mutual respect and regard. Investing time and energy in these relationships is critical. Colleagues often do like to help. We work with many people who have a great deal of experience and expertise, and they like to be called upon for that expertise. As highly social creatures, it's in our nature to want to share our abilities and contribute. By reaching out and asking for help, you are telling your colleagues that they have your respect and trust.

Let's step back from a challenge and consider how it can be compartmentalized and shared with others. Start with aspects of the problem that are not in your area of expertise. Who do you know in your network who has the expertise? Even better, who do you not know very well but could get to know by reaching out and sharing this opportunity to learn? It's a great way to deepen an emerging relationship. Ask that colleague about their area of expertise in a meaningful way. You may not be in a position of delegation and you don't have to be. Ask your questions humbly and seek the guidance and information you need.

If you are in a position to delegate, do that in a thoughtful way. Show your colleagues trust in asking for deliverables to help you complete what's needed. Be clear in what is being asked. Don't take on the world and convince yourself that you need to do it yourself and then get upset and resentful when overwhelmed. That is the bondage of self. Let go of it. Trust your network. Provide clear direction and expectations. Then guide your team to be successful in the delivery of their great work to you. Provide feedback, and of course, make corrections as needed along the way. Guide a team and savor its success. And when it is done, share the credit and say, "Thank you."

Delegating is a delicate art. When you delegate, you must let go and trust. Let the team, made up of delegates as well as those you can't delegate to but can engage with, chart their own course. It's not uncommon to fall into the trap of just doing it yourself because you can trust yourself to deliver. It takes a good deal of planning and organizing to delegate. Trusting colleagues is a big step. But, by relinquishing control, you gain so much strength. You gain the collective wisdom of everyone involved. Having your work benefit from input and collaboration from colleagues helps to improve the work and the experience.

Surrendering Control @ Work is about opening up to the power of a shared experience. Understanding that you are not at the center of every project nor are you responsible for every effort frees you up to have a collective experience with your network @ Work. Collaborate and set a vision. Delegate what makes sense and to whom it makes sense. Trust that your network will come through for you and provide the support the network needs. Help remove obstacles along the way. Provide meaningful and constructive feedback. Share the learning and successes and then move to the next experience.

ESTABLISHING YOUR SERENITY @ WORK

ONCE WE HAVE BEEN ABLE to truly surrender, we can start the journey and the work to establish our serenity. This process calls us to be honest with ourselves and with those in our lives. We need to be fearless in looking to self to identify our character defects and commit them to paper. What is within our make-up that drives us toward being reactionary, angry and centered on ourselves? You will benefit from being open to words that may feel uncomfortable at first but that capture your defects and allow you to consider them and improve. You are an active participant in earning your serenity.

When you look back on negative interactions at home and @ Work, what drove your behaviors? How did you contribute to the issue? Perhaps you were thinking solely of yourself. Maybe you were attacking, defensive, vengeful, selfish, jealous, petty, judgmental or bitter. In writing about this topic, these words came to me far too easily as the bigger hitters on my list of character defects. When I began the journey to assess my ownership and contribution to my unhappiness, I got to know those words very well. It was painful for me to think in those terms about myself, and painful to admit and write them down. But, it was also true and honest. It was cathartic. In considering my defects, I began to find release. By writing it all down, I could ponder them, size them up and take responsibility for them. Taking responsibility set the stage for me to forgive myself. Reflecting on this work, I see myself starting at the bottom of a large hill. I need to climb that hill because at the top I will have earned and found forgiveness. As I begin my climb, my character defects are a collection of boulders I need to climb over to make it to the top. Each boulder needs my attention. Each one needs to be considered, dealt with and surmounted. I need to know each one so I can understand how it impedes me. Below is my first attempt at recording and understanding my character defects early in this process. You may recognize some of these traits in yourself:

Self-Centered: Way too interested in what is in it for me. Put my needs first even though I am pretending or telling myself that I am putting others first.

Mean: Say and do terrible things when I am angry. Say things to be hurtful. Find someone's vulnerable area and attack. Say things I do not mean, in order to lash out.

Attacking: Go after those who I feel have hurt me. Talk about them in a destructive way.

Defensive: Unable to accept criticism, rejection or general feedback. Unless the feedback is positive, I get mean when given feedback. I accuse and get upset. Hurts my reputation, credibility and future. This has hurt me personally and professionally.

Selfish: I want what I what when I want it and care little for the impact on others. I am not always conscious of this, but it is so. I convince myself that I am all giving, but I am not. I give to get. I give and expect much in return. I give without being asked and then am angry when I do not get things in return. I say that I love unconditionally, but my conditions are great. I love on the condition that I am to get total loyalty in return. Anything in my estimation less than total loyalty is met with anger, resentment, and chastising.

Jealous: I am very jealous of others. I am jealous of those who I believe have more talent than I do. I am jealous of those who have more material comfort than I do. I am jealous of those in good relationships because I want that for myself.

Bitter/Resentful: I can't seem to let anything go. I hold on to pain and resentment constantly. I feel encased in bitterness. It's a shell around me that lets in little light. It has baked around me for 42 years. Layered and strong. I need to chip away at it.

Petty: When fueled by resentment, anger and bitterness, I pick at petty little things. I get caught up in comparing myself to others. I focus on my education and career as if to convince myself that I am superior to others.

Materialistic: I have put the acquisition of things ahead of my relationship with God. I have put it in front of my relationship with loved ones and personal/spiritual growth. I have been addicted to buying things as a way to fill a void within myself. I have expressed my love and tried to establish my value to others by giving material things rather than giving of myself. I have relied on having and buying things to define me and give me worth rather than finding value in myself, my being and my soul.

Judgmental: I have convinced myself that I am held to a higher standard. I allow myself to feel persecuted. I believe this drives me to judge everyone else. I judge education, intellect, and career. I put others down in my mind, believing it will make me feel better. The resulting negativity makes me feel bad about myself. It makes me feel guilty. I do not want to be the person who judges others. I want to be about positive things and positive affirmations.

Co-Dependent: I want to be wanted. I want to be needed. Too often, I define myself by who I am to others. Mom, daughter, wife and friend. I do not put enough stock into who I am on my own. I want to be adored externally, yet I have not figured out how to adore myself. Until I can, a healthy relationship is not possible.

Certainly, my defect list is very personal and digs into issues that are beyond the workplace. Why, then, do I include it here and believe it is relevant? Because, I don't believe it's possible to establish Serenity @ Work without acknowledging and embracing defects at the personal level. I found that when I was completely honest with myself and wrote all of these defects down, I was able to begin a journey of understanding that helped me to become my best and most authentic self in my personal life and @ Work. Your list may have similar or very different items. Perhaps your list is more about being impatient @ Work or too competitive. You need to consider those character defects that hold you back in finding your serenity.

Did I engage in these defects every day and in every interaction? Certainly not. But once I opened up to the exercise, I was all in. These character defects had played and continued to play a part in my unhappiness. I needed to call myself out on all of them. I needed to jump into the pool and swim around. The honesty was painful but also joyous. I no longer had to hide from these defects. I had owned up to them. They no longer skulked inside me. They were called out. They had names and they were mine. I could begin to deal with them.

Why insist on writing them down? Because we need to look at them and reflect on them. Having a physical record of these defects removes a certain mysterious power they had when we tried to hide from them and deny them. By labeling and defining my character defects, I took away their power and began to reduce their influence over me.

The next thing is to action this list. This begins with admitting our defects to someone. By sharing our character defects with another person, we take a large step toward freedom. We benefit by partnering with a trusted friend, family member, colleague, or counselor.

Then the hard part comes. A very difficult but wonderful part. We embrace and surrender to a higher power and ask that higher power to remove these defects. We cannot remove them by ourselves. We need to offer up our character defects. We need to surrender them to God, to the universe, to nature. Surrender them to a high power of our own understanding. I will not pretend that this just happens when we are ready and make the request. Being ready and asking are incredibly important. I have had to repeat this exercise over and over, again. I often find myself asking God to remove my defects. Each time, I find my defects diminishing. I become more and more free.

As I struggled with how cyclical this is for me, my sponsor shared an important perspective. She said, "We seldom completely get rid of our character defects. The trick is lessening their frequency and duration. You will find that you still develop resentments, but less and less often. And when you are in a resentment, you are able to resolve it and let it go much more quickly." Thanks be to God (that's me talking, you place reference to your higher power here), I have found this to be true.

Critical to earning your Serenity @ Work and at home is to acknowledge those you have hurt and make amends to them. Here is where it is important to be selfless. This journey is about you and your serenity, but it is critical that you do no harm to another by making your amends. So, if you have hurt someone, but telling them about it and apologizing to them will only cause them further pain, you need to take pause. An extreme example, that will make the point, is infidelity. Let's say a person wants to make an amends about having an affair with someone's spouse. If the spouse was never aware of the affair, it is not the right for anyone to cause him or her pain in the pursuit of serenity. Make the amends to self and to the high power, but leave it there.

Many amends do not fall into such a dangerous area. So, open up and think about those you may have harmed with your character defects. Have you been too competitive with a co-worker? Have you had a pattern of being quick to anger with a friend? Talk to them. Tell them you are sorry and are making efforts to not only stop the behavior but to grow past the drivers that have caused you to behave that way in the past. Not everyone will be open to the amends, but that is okay. If they can't accept your apology, wish them well from your heart and move on. Really move on. Allow yourself to release the guilt of what transpired and move forward. Once you have made your heartfelt amends, your side of the street is fresh and clean and beautiful. Forgive yourself. Value yourself. Love yourself.

I certainly needed to make a good deal of amends to a significant number of people in my life. Very memorable was the amends I made to my ex-partner, Paula. My drinking and character defects played a large role in our relationship ending after 12 years and a daughter together. As we built our separate lives after the break up, we still needed to interact a great deal as we were still raising our daughter. Our relationship remained mired in bitterness and resentment for a number of years. Through my work toward serenity, I realized how much I needed to make amends to her for the pain I caused her during our relationship. I needed to be open and honest with her about the part my defects and my drinking played in her pain. It was, by far, the hardest amends I had to make. I did not know if she would be able to hear the amends let alone accept them.

Paula was very surprised when I approached her and apologized for the pain my drinking had caused her. At first, she was very quiet as she absorbed what I had said. Here response was simple. She looked at me and said, "Thank you." There were a great number of feelings packed into that statement of thanks. More words were not necessary, as I understood everything that was behind those two words. I cried, she cried and we were both free.

Prior to working on my character defects, my life seemed to be driven by fear, resentment and an inability to be honest with myself. Through the process of working on my character defects and making amends, I found honesty, vulnerability and grace to be the main tenets of my emerging serenity. I say emerging as I still have work to do, but the work makes sense to me and feeds a calmness in my personal and professional life.

THE FREEDOM OF FORGIVENESS @ WORK

AS I WORKED TO ESTABLISH a measure of serenity, I found that old resentments were holding me back. They were in control of my life. I was open to surrendering control of my life to my higher power, but had to admit to myself that these resentments were still too powerful in my life. As a result, I was stuck and could not be free to embrace serenity.

One of the most helpful things I have ever heard at an AA Meeting is, "Forgiving someone does not make the thing that happened okay." That is very important to keep in mind. Many of us have hurts that can't ever be perceived as okay. They are simply too devastating. But to forgive the one who hurt us, that is what we seek to do. In forgiving, we set ourselves free. We take away the power of the thing that happened and we take away the impact the person who did it still has on our lives. If you are resentful of someone who hurt you, they are still occupying space in your head that they do not deserve. Free that space up. Let go of that resentment! But, how? How do you do that?

The Big Book of Alcoholics Anonymous talks about the need to think about the person or people toward whom you hold resentments and pray for them to have every blessing. Pray for them to have peace, good fortune and serenity in their lives. This is so hard to do. I have always struggled to forgive those who have hurt me. I still struggle. I rely heavily on the "Fake it 'til you make it," approach on this. I have prayed for people to have great things in their lives even though my heart was not in it. Then I prayed again and again until I meant it. I pray for them but I also pray for myself. Forgiving them and praying for good things in their lives frees me of the weight of resentment. I value that freedom dearly and need to work toward it daily. I became so tired of carrying around that heavy chain of resentment. Every time I pray and gain perspective, another link falls from that chain. It is still there, but it is getting smaller and lighter all the time. And I am lighter. There are times when I regress and forge a new link or two. But I soon return to the process of forgiveness and move forward.

Striving to be selfless and forgiving is the greatest gift you can give yourself. You declare your freedom from the bindings of anger, of fear and of resentment. These negative feelings feed off of your soul. They deplete you of your essence. Forgiveness frees, feeds and fortifies.

When I began this journey toward serenity, I had to dig deep to identify who I needed to forgive and why. Early in my sobriety, I was working with a therapist and we discussed latent pain I was feeling over a family tragedy that was, at that time, 40 years in the past. When I was three years old, my eight-year-old sister, Karen, died. Her death shattered our family and set the stage for my mother to descend into alcoholism. I watched as my parents justified a great deal of drinking and bad choices. I saw a pattern that suited me well many years later when my life was dealt hard and unfair blows. Karen's death was a reason to drink. My daughter's autism was a reason to drink. The bad hands dealt to me where all reasons why I needed and deserved to drink.

If I were to stay sober, I needed to deal with this pain. I needed to take away its power. I needed to forgive. I needed to examine my mom's part in all this and try to understand what was behind the behavior. I had to develop a perspective that did not leave me angry and resentful.

My counselor and I decided that to deal with all of these feelings I needed to open up to my mom and to myself. In 2009, when I wrote the letter that follows, my mom was still alive. I wrote it to her but the letter was really for me. She never read this letter because I never asked her to. She did not know it existed. That was because I knew she could not handle its content or gain anything positive from it. I had no intention of pushing her into a conversation she simply could not have. Again, serenity cannot be established at the expense of anyone else. It is key to address issues with others so far as you can without doing harm to them. This journey was for me and helped me. I had neither the right nor the inclination to cause her pain. I was able to take this action and benefit from it but I did not have to involve my mom even though she was central to it. Why? Because she is central to my experience. I can talk and I can write about her and be open with my feelings, and I can hold up how her actions affected me. But if she would not benefit, I needed to not pull her in. So I didn't. Yet this exercise did for me a world of good. I extracted pain that had held me back from serenity. I took away that pain's power. I began to clean a slate that would allow me to get in touch with my true self and not be encumbered with resentment. Here is the letter:

* * *

Mom –

I understand why you had so much rage. You were raised in an atmosphere of anger, abuse and neglect. As with many women of your generation, you sought to find peace, happiness and home by finding a good husband and having a family. For many women that is a wonderful dream that can turn into a fabulous life.

You went forward in that dream with a man who was not good. Your low self-esteem and need to get out of your unhappy life allowed you to marry a bad man who was mean and abusive to you. You were not even safe in your pregnancy as he beat you and caused an early labor in the sixth month. You had to leave him and you ended up right back in a house with your mother. Only this time, you also had to deal with the label of "Single Parent Divorcee". In rural Pennsylvania in the 1950's, that label was synonymous with "whore".

The life you had dreamed about was now so out of reach. You put that dream away and moved on as best you could. Then my dad came along. He too had been hurt and humiliated by a failed first marriage. He instantly fell in love and pursued you. When you married him, it seemed, at last, that your turn at a beautiful life was at hand.

With the births of Michele and Karen, you had a beautiful family and moved to the Long Island suburbs with the other young families struggling to make ends meet but enjoying the journey full of family, good neighbors and love. A few years later, a surprise pregnancy rounded out the family with another little girl. You had your brood of four and a husband who adored you.

But pain found you again. Karen was always a sick little girl. Her asthma was such that she was limited in how much she could play. You were the only one who saw the really bad attacks, and as a result, many in your support system thought you were over reacting to Karen's condition. They just didn't understand how bad is really was.

When they finally saw a bad attack, it was the last one. At eight years old, that beautiful little girl was taken. With her, you and dad in large part died too. It was just too much for you to take. For an all too brief shining moment you had had your Camelot. When part of it was taken away, you felt the need to let it die altogether. Our family withered. We were six, then five but never one.

You lingered on Long Island for a couple of years but the memories were too painful. You did not find enough peace in being surrounded by friends and family to stay.

We left Long Island and left our lives, our culture, our touchstone. The bitter loneliness you felt in your heart after Karen's death became our reality in all aspects of our lives. We lived as individuals in Pennsylvania. We all tried to find our own ways to cope. You drank, dad got a girlfriend, Michele initially got in with a tough crowd and I learned to play alone.

I'm pretty sure my aversion to solitude began then. I simply did not have a choice in being alone. It had nothing to do with what I wanted. If you played alone and were alone, it was because no one else wanted you. No one valued you. No one loved you. These were my perceptions and I internalized them. I should not have. I was a good little kid who had done nothing wrong to cause my loneliness. My being alone was a circumstance. It was not a result of any personal failing.

On Long Island, Jerry got a lot of dad's anger, but I was a bit too young to remember much. But I do remember Michele getting the brunt of Dad's anger and yours. That made me angry and protective. I swore I would take care of Michele. Seems that was the start of my "Knight in Shining Armor Complex," which has led me to try to save my partners prior to sobriety.

I need to forgive you. First I need to tell you how you hurt me. You yelled at me and hit me when you were drunk. You scared me because I didn't know then that you were drunk. I was too young to understand what being drunk was and led to it. I thought you were having bad moods and I couldn't understand where they came from. You were not my mom when you were like that. You were strange and scary and I could not reach you. My safety and security vanished when a "mood" came.

I remember a cloudy day on Long Island when I was five. All the older kids were in school. You locked me out of the house. I knocked on the door and called for you but you told me to "Go away." I could see you but I couldn't get in. All the other smalls and kids' moms were nowhere to be seen. The houses and streets were empty. Where was everyone? It was weird and scary. It was chilly and cloudy and I could see you through the window, but I couldn't get in. I know now that you were drinking and needed space. But at my age I couldn't comprehend that. I thought I had done something wrong.

Drunk or sober, if I did something wrong, the emotional punishment was severe. You yelled and glared, then gave me the silent treatment. If I wasn't perfect, you took your love away. I had to figuratively crawl and beg to get it back. It wasn't my fault. I was just a kid. I fought and scraped for a kind of love that had ceased to exist. You could never love fully after Karen died.

There is no need for blame. There is nothing to gain from blame. It just was. And it is over. I do not need to keep this. I can forgive. I can release. I can open myself up to love and beauty and vulnerability. I can celebrate my relationships for what they are and not what I want them to be. There is no future in taking broken people and trying to fix them with my love. It did not work then, and it will not work now. My worth is not measured by how happy I make an unhappy person. My happiness comes from inner peace, my relationship with God and my unconditional love for my daughter, Talia.

I've stopped blaming myself. Now, finally, I can forgive you. You were sad and devastated and broken. When you loved beautifully, it was taken away. You needed to love cautiously and conditionally so that if another irreplaceable treasure was taken away, your soul would not be shattered to oblivion. I understand you, I love you and I forgive you.

Love,

Maureen

* * *

Writing that letter gave me a voice for my pain. It gave me a forum to reflect on my understanding of what drove the behaviors in my childhood that laid a foundation for unhappiness and self-destructive behavior. Thinking about it, writing it down and forgiving was such a powerful experience. It encouraged me to take a next step to deal with another complicated relationship in my life: my older sister, Michele. During this same period of work and healing in 2009, I wrote the following letter to her:

* * *

Michele –

It was very hard for you growing up. You and Karen were so close in so many ways. Just 18 months your junior, Karen was your little sister and best friend. I can't imagine your pain and confusion when she was taken. While I have no way of knowing for certain, I can imagine that your feelings and trauma were never fully acknowledged or dealt with as our mother has always treated the tragedy as her exclusive cross to bear.

You initially felt the pain of our move from Long Island much more than I did. You were embarking on adolescence and placed into a new and unfamiliar setting. While I was too young to understand, you recognized mom's alcoholism from the start. As such, you were forced to deal with it alone as a mere 12-year-old.

Jerry was mom's pampered son, I was the indulged "Little One" and you were relegated to middle child. You bore the brunt of a great deal of the emotional abuse from mom and dad. I think that when you found, fell in love with and married Joe, you were so ready to build the family and life that had eluded you as a child. You have succeeded in every way. I fear that being close to me causes you too much pain. The memories I conjure and the life I represent are just too painful for you to face. For that reason, you push me away and are dismissive of me.

I also think that you had to deal with too much drama in your life prior to adulthood. That is why you don't want to deal with me being gay or any of the issues I deal with.

When I ended a 12-year relationship with Paula, you were not always there for me. I would call needing to talk about it. If you were in the mood, we would have a good talk. That made it worse for the times when you would turn a cold ear. Those are the times that made me feel unlovable and not worth anyone's time. I have scars on my heart from you doing that to me. I don't think it's because you don't love me. It's because sometimes you don't want to deal with me. You want the life you have worked so hard to build. You are tired of the shame and frustration that our family has caused you your entire life. I need to keep in mind that your rejection is not about me. It's about your understandable need to have peace and happiness in your life. I understand – finally. I love you. I support you and I forgive you.

Love,

Maureen

* * *

As with the letter to my mom, I did not send this letter to my sister. We were estranged at the time and I knew that direct contact was not advisable. What I did not know and was so happy to realize a few years later is that my sister was going through her own evolution. When my mother died in 2012, we saw each other for the first time in seven years and we slowly began to rebuild a relationship. Michele reached a point where she could not only acknowledge my sexuality but embrace it. She was my matron of honor at my wedding to Dinah in 2013 and we now enjoy a warm and supportive relationship. I needed to not only deal with my feelings and forgive, but I also needed to give her space and patience to grow to where she needed to be.

I continued the exercise of looking to myself and dealing with the open wounds. My counselor helped me realize that I had one more letter to write. We knew that on some level I needed to forgive Karen for leaving us and what that did to our family. I also needed to forgive myself for feeling anger toward an innocent child and holding a resentment toward Karen that she did not deserve. I wrote the following letter to Karen forty years after we had lost her:

* * *

Karen –

It's hard to write to someone who is such a stranger to me. I have no memory of you. I have precious little information about you as the stories are few and far between. Who are you to me? Even if you are just a concept, you are beloved and dear to me. I have felt your absence my entire conscious life. I have longed to remember and know you. I have great anger over not knowing you. I had peers exactly my age who remembered you. Hearing them tell me stories about us all together, when we were small, caused me great anger and resentment at the time.

As I grew up, I grew resentful of you. That resentment caused me a great deal of guilt. How could I resent the memory of a little girl who suffered on earth and was taken so soon? What kind of person, what kind of sister resents that? I guess one who was hurt and confused and wanting an answer for why there was so much loneliness.

In some sad interpretation of the world, I've always needed to find a source of blame. Often that source was me. Right or wrong, I have blamed myself, our parents, our sister and even you for the pain I felt growing up and pain that lingers still. What I am finally realizing is that there is no blame, no fault, and no retribution to be paid. It just was. You dying was not fair. What it did to our family was not fair. What it did to me was not fair. But, it wasn't anyone's fault. It wasn't God's fault, either. It just was. And it is over. My love for you will never leave. I know the day will come when we will all be together in Heaven. Until then, I pray that you rest in God's piece and know that your little sister loves you. She no longer blames you or resents you. We are both free.

Love,

Maureen

* * *

Writing this letter established, for me, a good deal of freedom. It released me and Karen from this anger and resentment. The love and the feeling of loss are still there, but I no longer feel enveloped in the tragedy. What I had to realize is that I could acknowledge the sadness and the pain of Karen's loss without having to focus on just the death. There had been a life and it was beautiful. Her presence was wonderful and touched our world in a positive way. Karen had always been presented to me as a symbol of my mom's suffering. I've no doubt of how destructive the death of a child can be to a parent. I have never doubted that it must be the worst loss possible. However, with my mom, that story only had one note. The note of devastation, aftermath, a point of no return. My mom could not see Karen as anything else but the source of her life's greatest tragedy. What was lost, as a result, was the dignity of this child's life and the gift she had been to our family.

For that reason, I so respected my sister, Michele, for a story she told at a family dinner. I was visiting the whole family in Pennsylvania. My sister, her husband and three kids along with my mom and my daughter were together for a rare visit. My sister started telling the cutest story about Karen and her when they were very small. Michele and Karen were playing with their Barbies and somehow Michele had traded a single Barbie for all of Karen's Barbie clothes. So Karen was left with an extra Barbie and no clothes for any of the dolls. She had been swindled and tears followed. Michele told the story with a smile and chuckle and I had such joy in watching her children hear a story about Karen that was cute and fun and full of childhood mischievousness.

I've always loved and admired Michele, but in that moment she was my hero. Her story brought back dignity to Karen's memory. She transformed Karen from a sad and somewhat taboo subject to a figure of love and joy in our family history. What a gift she gave to me that day and what a gift she has given to her children. She taught me to look at Karen's life and her impact from all dimensions. Yes, there is sadness and anger and pain. There is also beauty and love and joy.

What I have focused on in this chapter is deeply personal, but it has a place in recognizing that Forgiveness is Freedom @ Work. My letters are about a journey of trying to look at people, circumstances, and the pain they cause us from their perspective. I needed to address this pain so I could establish serenity in all aspects of my life. This journey has helped me in both my personal and professional life. Serenity transcends into every part of who we are.

We are deeply impacted by our colleagues. We enter into professional relationships trying to establish credibility and trust. When we are disappointed or betrayed in those relationships, we are easily hurt personally as well as professionally.

In professional settings, I find it helpful to try to understand the perspective and journey of a colleague who is causing me resentment. This has helped me to have and show grace where I would otherwise react and allow my anger, though justified, to harm me and my professional brand. The ability to find grace and to genuinely forgive has helped me improve relationships and grow professionally. My first exercises in how to forgive were steeped in my most personal and intimate pain. Having worked through those feelings helps me address the hurts and frustrations @ Work with a confidence that I can successfully forgive and be my most authentic self @ Work.

FAKE IT 'TIL YOU MAKE IT @ WORK

I HAVE ALREADY USED THE "Fake it 'til you make it" phrase and here it is again. I find great wisdom in the statement. I do not mean to lie and put your ethics as risk. Instead, I am encouraging you to think and act "As If ." When it comes to Serenity @ Work, I believe it is critical to approach things as if you are at peace. Fake your serenity until it becomes real. Once I got sober, I did not even realize I was doing this, but I was.

Let me make my point with a personal example, as I believe it applies in spades here. My family often dealt with the challenges and pain of life by lying to themselves and others about what really happened, how it affected them and most importantly how it affected those around them. Most members of my family did this to protect themselves from having to face pain felt or pain caused.

My brother, Jerry, God rest his soul, did this to protect himself from facing his pain. Jerry was the product of my mother's first marriage that ended in divorce. In 1960, my mom met my dad and the two were married when Jerry was nine. I believe my dad's intentions were good but he just did not have it in him to raise, with grace, a child that was not his. As we three girls came along, Jerry's status in the family became that much more devalued. It is hard to decipher truth from fiction in the family stories, but my brother was convinced that when we moved from Long Island to Pennsylvania in 1974, my parents did not mention that they had a son in college back in New York. They simply presented our family as comprising just two daughters. Karen was gone and Jerry simply did not exist. Jerry told me that when he came to visit us for the first time, he quickly realized while talking with a neighbor that the neighbor did not know he was part of the family. In fact, the neighbor thought me mentioning my big brother was just a five year old having a fun and active imagination. I suspect it was a weird conversation for all involved.

Jerry told me that he confronted my father and asked why he would do such a thing. My father simply responded that he and my mom wanted a fresh start with "their" kids. Ouch. My brother told me he bought a coffee mug with the name of that new town we moved to and kept it as a reminder of this incident. I do not know if this is true, but to my brother and to his inner soul, it was true and it hurt.

Fast forward 40 years. My brother and I were driving from my mother's funeral mass outside of Pittsburgh to the Philadelphia area where she was to be buried next to my dad who had died 19 years before. As we traversed the Pennsylvania Turnpike, we talked about a number of things. The topic of our move back in 1974 came up and that is when I learned about the mug—that sad talisman to an act of betrayal that stung Jerry so deeply. As my mom had just died, we naturally talked about the events around my dad's death. My brother recalled a version of events that both saddened my heart and scared me to my core.

Jerry recounted how he had given my father his last bath and that my father died in his arms while Jerry combed my father's hair. This did not happen. I gently reminded my brother that my dad was very weak at the end and did not leave the hospital bed that was set up for him in our house. That hospital bed had been in our living room on the first floor for at least two days before he died. The full bathroom with a tub was on the second floor and no one would have carried this suffering man up a flight of stairs for a bath. Jerry pushed back and said that he had, at least, crawled in bed with my dad and held him as he died. I could tell that Jerry was getting upset. I needed to give him this one.

The surprising thing to me is that in that moment I did not feel anger. I felt sadness. I felt pity and great fear. I felt fear in the power we have over each other to cause such pain. Jerry had been made to feel so flawed, so broken and so unworthy of love that he needed to take the source of those feelings, our father, and create this vision of deep and lasting love in my dad's final moments. He needed to create that and I needed to let him.

The old me. The old me who did not know serenity but only knew resentment and rage would have taken the lie and smoldered on it for a long time. I would have stopped the conversation and insisted that the "truth be told and respected." But I was different now. I had grown. I stopped and let him believe the lie because I felt true pity and compassion. Jerry needed this lie because he needed to feel that important to our father.

I had the luxury of knowing that my father loved me. My father adored his girls. We were the smartest, the prettiest and the best daughters ever. He gave that to me. But for Jerry, he had no father's pride to offer. For all of the mistakes my parents made, they gave me a foundation of parental pride from which to start my life. The fact that my brother faced life without that base brings me sorrow.

In that exchange during our drive, I gave my brother a gift of which I am sure he was not aware. He was able to see himself in that fantasy and derive comfort from it. Jerry gave me a gift that day, too. He gave me freedom. I finally felt free from the need to "correct" the family history. I was able to know grace. The details were not as important as the human need. I was able to trade the importance of my family "facing the facts" for the importance of Jerry having his peace. Jerry was just trying to survive. I found peace in giving him the love and support he needed in that moment. That event gave me a level of trust in my serenity that guided me into compassion. Beyond acting "as if," I was able to show true grace.

Having these experiences in my personal life made it so much easier to do the same in my professional life. I am certainly not advocating that you allow a colleague to perpetuate a harmful lie just to keep the peace. Rather, seek to understand the subtext of a given situation and strive for compassion along with integrity. Is it really so important to be right or is it better to ensure the right thing happens? Do you need to dissect who was right and who was wrong in the exchange? Probably not. I have often said, "Being right is not worth it if you look back and see bodies in the road." Lead with compassion, integrity and good will. Fake that until it feels right. It will feel right faster than you think and you will be fulfilled by the strength compassion gives your soul.

MAINTAINING YOUR SERENITY @ WORK

WHEN YOU START TO FEEL the peace and joy that comes from serenity both at home and @ Work, it is truly wonderful. It is such a joy to view life through lenses unclouded by old resentments and character defects. However, the novelty of this new feeling does have a way of wearing off. Also, external factors like challenging co-workers, competing demands and lack of time are still in play. They are a constant threat to our serenity. Not because anyone is out to injure us or undo the work, but because the people and circumstances in our lives are complicated, messy and amazing. Our ongoing quest is to keep the serenity we have established. Like a well-loved child, serenity needs to be nurtured and allowed to grow.

The question of how to keep our serenity deserves a good deal of consideration. Our character defect work and amends are two of our fiercest tools to help us nurture and preserve our serenity. When you find at home or @ Work that you have wronged someone, call it out and make the amends. Avoid that cycle of defensiveness and guilt that held you down before. Know that your character defects are still part of you. Every time you recognize a character defect and ask your higher power to remove it, you fortify your serenity. Every time you make heartfelt amends to someone, you strengthen your serenity. Standing in your truth makes you strong. Even if your truth is to humbly admit that you were, in that situation, wrong. That recognition and that act gives you power.

I love that humility and power come together. I believe it is a mistake to equate humility with weakness. Humility comes from a place of confidence and courage. When we look to ourselves for approval rather than others, there is no need for defensiveness and self-preservation. It takes a great deal of belief in self to let go and be humble. It is the very definition of strength.

What about when someone hurts you? As much as humility makes us powerful, so does forgiveness. We have come to know that we simply cannot control the actions of others. Our colleagues will move forward on their journey driven by their strengths, weaknesses and the impact of their experiences. We cannot control that. We do have the gift of owning our reactions. When we approach with humility and grace, we contribute to our serenity. We also model, for all involved, a measured and emotionally intelligent way to deal with a challenging situation or colleague. When we approach a situation in a constructive way, we provide a blueprint for dealing with tough circumstances in a productive way. Backing down without a good result helps no more than burning bridges. Pointing out a way forward in a direct and reasonable manner helps us to move the situation, the team and organization forward. We act as a true leader. Leadership is about much more than formal power. Great leaders demonstrate behaviors from which others can benefit and grow.

Especially @ Work, you can be right and you can call that colleague out for the infraction. However, being right just isn't enough. To be a true leader, you need to look at the event from the other person's perspective and try to empathize with him or her. Certainly, fix the business problem. Just do it with grace and see what can be learned from it. You may be the only one learning, but that is okay. You focus on your journey. He or she focuses on theirs. If, however, you are in a position to provide feedback @ Work, deliver it in the true spirit of helping your colleague to grow and be their best and most authentic self.

When faced with a thorny problem @ Work, we often let the problem fester, fueled by our disbelief and anger. The problem at hand can center on a genuine business question. These are usually straightforward. That is until personalities become involved. And, personalities always get involved. We have all come across interpersonal challenges in the workplace. It is very common to encounter people in our day to day who are challenging for us to work with. We can spend a great deal of time thinking about how they could be and should be different. And we can count on NO HANDS the number of times our opinion of how a challenging person should act has had an actual impact on how they do act. We cannot control others; we can only control our reactions.

Working on the solution and not on the problem requires us to transcend the emotions of the problem. Emotions are the trap here. We cannot change our situation by focusing on how unfortunate or unfair the situation is. We gain strength and possibility when we think in terms of what we can do to have a positive impact on the situation. What steps can we take to make the situation better?

I once worked on a project turnaround as a project lead in a consulting capacity. The team was weighed down by a great deal of dysfunction in the form of territorial fighting and resistance to collaboration. The drivers of this disharmony were the feelings of the people involved in the project. The problem was not the technology, timeline or funding. The problem was a lack of trust across the team.

I certainly thought more than once that life would be so much easier if those involved in the team would simply leave ego at the door and get on with it. While this sentiment was most likely accurate, it would do nothing to solve the issues at hand. It was also an egotistical assessment on my part. So, there is that.

In this situation, it was critical to try to understand the cause for the lack of trust rather than focus on the fact that it should not have been there at all. It is also important to understand the frames of reference of those on the team. I had to quickly step outside the problem. I needed to stop focusing on the fact that the team issue should not have been happening in the first place. The fact was that disharmony was present and the project was in jeopardy as a result.

One of the biggest issues for this team was that they were focusing on personalities and not facts. What I felt was the biggest weakness gave me the recipe to find the solution. I relied on the facts. To the best of my ability, I tried to understand the history of the members of the team and how that history impacted their current view. Often, if those involved in an area seem territorial and inflexible, it is because they were instrumental in solving a past problem or problems and helping the organization to find success. That is difficult to let go of when a business solution calls for a change to what has been in place. This was the situation I observed. Members of the team who had provided a solution that had worked for a long time were being asked to work with outside consultants to replace that very work. In doing so, the organization was pushing aside technology and processes that had been a source of pride for quite some time.

Notice that when I write about this I am not avoiding the use of personal and, frankly, emotional prose. Work can be personal as it calls for us to invest a good deal of ourselves into it. Why ignore that? Celebrate it! The moment I acknowledged that these team members had invested in the current process and honored their emotional investment, I was able to begin to build the trust necessary to help them embrace the new direction.

These team members were living in the problem as they saw it. Their tried and true technology and process was being replaced. The fact was, though, the old technology and processes were not tried and true. Their approach was flawed and in need of constant care to ensure accurate output. What the team felt was that the very care and diligence they had invested in with pride for many years was being tossed aside. A part of their legacy was being discarded. Given the personal nature of professional investment, it was perfectly understandable that this situation felt hurtful.

For the external consultant side of the fence, they had lovingly built a best-in-class technical solution that they were proud to implement. The tricky balance was to acknowledge the expertise within the internal team that would be instrumental in making the new technology successful. A partnership between the tenured expertise and the new technology was essential for the organization to be successful. Every member of the team, both internal and consultant, was critical to achieving the desired result.

We found the answer in acknowledging what was being retired. We discussed as a team the sense of loss. We outlined the extra work the team needed to engage in every day to make the present solution viable. The new technology would help the team avoid these extra steps and ensure quality. By outlining the details of the new solution's positive impacts, we created an appetite for the new system. We made it clear that both the internal team and the consultants would be key to a successful implementation. A partnership was forged. The partnership included shared goals, shared pain and shared success. We had to deal with the personal hurdles to attain professional success.

BE OF SERVICE @ WORK

MY HOPE IS THAT WE have come to recognize that truth, selflessness and humility are tenets of serenity. These qualities of serenity call us into the action of service. By serving others, we stand our best chance of maintaining our serenity. This is especially true @ Work where opportunities to serve are many. The colleagues we interact with every day benefit from the application of our experience and expertise to serve as leaders and guides.

Consider how Servant Leadership works with the idea of Serenity @ Work. The term "servant leadership" was put forth by Robert Greenleaf. Greenleaf explains that the servant leader is a servant first. Service Leadership begins with the natural feeling that the leader wants to serve. That conscious choice to serve draws us to aspire to lead. Power and influence are gained but are not the focus. Power and influence are byproducts of serving.

The old autocratic way of leading teams and individuals has really become outdated and that is a good thing. Approaching a team with the idea that you are a leader either by direct reporting authority or even by virtue of leading a project fails to motivate. To truly energize teams @ Work, it is so much more effective to lead with service in mind.

We serve a good number of people @ Work. We serve our customers both internal and external. We serve our teammates and we serve those who report to us. And, of course, we serve our direct leader. Service does not mean we need to be subservient. On the contrary, we often need to engage in constructive confrontation to provide our best service.

To serve is to put the needs of others first. We need to serve the best interests of our teammates and the organization. They need our expertise and ability to move the organization and team forward. The key is to drive forward unburdened by our own ambitions and ego. Moving forward with the good of others in mind frees us from being encumbered by selfishness.

What drives this service? What makes us want to put the needs of others first? Love drives us. I suspect this sounds very strange in a work context. If I asked you to approach everyone @ Work with love, that might feel very uncomfortable. The love I am talking about is different from our traditional definition of love rooted in affection, passion and devotion. I am referring to a love centered in benevolence and charity. It is universal and unconditional. It's called agape love. Agape love focuses on faithfulness, commitment and good will. When we open ourselves to love our colleagues and clients, we are driven by a genuine interest in putting their needs before our own in every circumstance. Our need to achieve solely for personal and professional gain will give way to a call to bring our best work forth to serve others and to serve the goals of our teams.

Even if we do not realize it, our actions will serve as an example to those with whom we work. We influence those around us with both our positive and negative actions. By demonstrating a mission of service in our work, our spirit can influence those around us to adopt a similar approach. Team dynamics do not just happen. They evolve from the interactions that take place amongst the team. When the actions of a team are driven by patience, kindness, humility, respect and honesty, team members will be positioned to do their best work.

I once worked with an amazing leader who explained in a town hall that if 20% of our projects did not fail, we were not trying hard enough to innovate. That was an exciting message. She knew that to transform, we needed to push the boundaries. You cannot do that if you are afraid to fail. It is like playing chess. When I was a kid, I always played chess to "not lose." While I was busy protecting my queen, my brother would sacrifice his queen and take all my other pieces. I would leave myself with a queen, king and a couple of rooks running around the board while he cornered my king with all of his other pieces. You need to take chances to win. You and the members of the team need to feel safe with each other so that risks are taken and lessons learned.

Fear is one the of the greatest threats to Serenity @ Work. Removing fear and promoting trust moves the entire ecosystem toward a positive and productive environment. In an atmosphere of safety and trust, risks are taken and breakthroughs made.

SET BOUNDARIES @ WORK

JUST TO KEEP YOU ON your toes, I am going to follow that chapter about service with one dedicated to setting boundaries. This may seem counterintuitive but it really is not. There are times when you best serve your colleagues, leaders and business partners by saying, "No." You are in the position you have @ Work because you have talent, expertise and a professional brand. Those with whom you work need you to bring the best parts of your ability to your work. In that spirit, there are times when you need to push back, ensure your ideas are heard and understood.

In a previous role, I was a Chief of Staff supporting a high-ranking Vice President. I was to help him run his organization. I worked on his town hall and newsletter messaging. I put action plans in place to respond to feedback on employee surveys. He often asked me to research and take action on a number of business and team initiatives. Once, I struggled to reconcile what he was asking me to do with the business issue at hand. I felt I was entering an unproductive black hole. I respectfully asked him to pause and explain to me what business problem he was trying to solve. When he outlined it in more detail, I explained that I believed his course of action would not be effective and offered an alternative. I was nervous to do this as I was relatively new to my position and our relationship was nascent.

To my delight, he thanked me not just for the superior approach but also for being candid and for sharing my professional opinion. This was refreshing for him because as he climbed the organizational ladder, he was noticing that team members were less likely to challenge him. To his credit, he invited productive discourse to move the organization forward.

That was a leader moment. What about clients? We all have clients. They may be external clients that we serve based on a formal contract, or internal clients that we serve based on an organization's business partnerships. In either relationship, we are meant to help our clients solve complex business problems or build new business solutions. They look to us to be experts in our field. The minute you compromise your expertise to acquiesce to their demands without question, you quickly descend from trusted advisor to order-taker. To be effective, it is critical to be able to say, "No" when necessary and deliver on your professional brand.

WHAT HAPPENS NEXT?

MY HOPE IN WRITING THIS book is to share my journey toward Surrendering Control, Establishing and Maintaining Serenity @ Work. I've reflected on my journey in this process through my character defect inventory, forgiveness letters and stories. You too can take this journey. I have put together a companion piece to provide exercises to guide readers through the process and benefit from the work. The core goals are to Surrender Control, Establish and Maintain Serenity @ Work. The workbook is called the Serenity @ Work(book).

www.ingramcontent.com/pod-product-compliance
Lightning Source LLC
Chambersburg PA
CBHW030004050426
42451CB00006B/107